THE VALUE OF

TIME
IN
THE
MUSLIM'S LIFE

SHAYKH ABDUR RAZZAAQ BIN ABD-MUHSIN AL-BADR

ISBN: 978-1-9432-7728-5

First Edition: Shaban 1436 A.H./May 2015 C.E.

Cover Design: Aboo Sulaymaan Muhammad Abdul-Azim bin Joshua Baker

Translation by Mostafa Abdul-Hakim Muhammad Lameu
Revised & Editing by Maktabatulirshad Staff

Typesetting & Formatting by Aboo Sulaymaan Muhammad Abdul-Azim bin Joshua Baker

Printing: Ohio Printing

Subject: Admonition

Website: www.maktabatulirshad.com
E-mail: info@maktabatulirshad.com

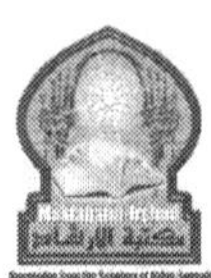

Table of Contents

BRIEF BIOGRAPHY OF THE AUTHOR

His name: Shaykh Abdur Razzaaq Bin Abd-Muhsin Al-Badr.

He is the son of Al-'Allamah Muhaddith of Medina Shaykh 'Abdul-Muhsin Al-'Abbad Al-Badr.

Birth: He was born on the 22nd day of Dhul-Qaddah in the year 1382 AH in az-Zal'fi, Kingdom of Saudia Arabia. He currently resides in Al-Medina Al-Munawwarah.

Current occupation: He is a member of the teaching staff in the Islamic University, in Al-Medina.

Scholastic certifications: Doctorate in Aqeedah.

The Shaykh has authored books, research, as well as numerous explanations in different sciences. Among them:

1. Fiqh of Supplications & Ad-Dhkaar.

2. Hajj & refinement of Souls,

3. Explanation of the book "Exemplary Principles" By Shaykh Uthaymeen (May Allah have mercy upon him).

4. Explanation of the book "the principles of Names & Attributes" authored by Shaykh-ul-Islam Ibnul-Qayyim (May Allah have mercy upon him).

5. Explanation of the book "Good Words" authored by Shaykh-ul-Islam Ibn Qayyim (May Allah have mercy upon him).

6. Explanation of the book "Aqeedah Tahaawiyyah".

7. Explanation of the book "Fusuul: Biography of the Messenger) By Ibn Katheer (May Allah have mercy upon him).

8. He has a full explanation of the book "Aadaab-ul-Muf'rad" authored by Imam Bukhari (May Allah have mercy upon him).

From the most distinguished scholars whom he has taken knowledge and acquired knowledge from are:

1. His father Al-'Allamah Shaykh 'Abdul-Muhsin Al-Badr — may Allah preserve him.

2. Al-'Allamah Shaykh Ibn Baaz — may Allah have mercy upon him.

3. Al-'Allamah Shaykh Muhammad Bin Saleh Al-'Uthaymeen — may Allah have mercy upon him.

4. Shaykh Ali Nasir Faqeehi — may Allah preserve him.

INTRODUCTION

In the Name of Allah, the Most Gracious, the Most Merciful

Dear brothers, I start with greeting you with the official greeting of Islam, namely, peace be upon you. I beseech Allah for you to benefit from this meeting and make it good and blessed.

At the beginning of this session about the value of time in the Muslim's life, I pray to Allah with the Duaa authenticated by Imam Muslim on the authority of Abu Huraira رضي الله عنه that the Prophet (ﷺ) was supplicating:

اللَّهُمَّ أَصْلِحْ لِي دِينِي الَّذِي هُوَ عِصْمَةُ أَمْرِي، وَأَصْلِحْ لِي دُنْيَايَ الَّتِي فِيهَا مَعَاشِي، وَأَصْلِحْ لِي آخِرَتِي الَّتِي فِيهَا مَعَادِي، وَاجْعَلِ الْحَيَاةَ زِيَادَةً لِي فِي كُلِّ خَيْرٍ، وَاجْعَلِ الْمَوْتَ رَاحَةً لِي مِنْ كُلِّ شَرٍّ

"The Messenger of Allah (ﷺ) used to say: "(O Allah, make my religion easy for me by which my affairs are protected, set right for me my world where my life exists, make good for me my Hereafter which is my resort, and which I have to return and make my life performing all types of good, and make death a comfort for me from evil)."

Brothers, this Duaa, contains all kinds of goodness and includes all sorts of advantages in this life and the one to come. This significant supplication clearly indicates the dire need of the servant to Allah's help, His success and correctness. The uprightness of your religion, life, and the Hereafter is solely dependent on Allah's help for you to do so. The absence of this help from Allah, however, results in the total opposite of the earlier. So the servant is essentially in the need for Allah to set straight his faith, life, and the afterlife. This Duaa includes all kinds of good **"set right my religion, set right my life and set right my afterlife"** this is the supplication of the Prophet Muhammad (ﷺ).

Whenever the Muslim mentions this Duaa, he must practice and take the measures as the Prophet (ﷺ) said:

اِحْـرِصْ عَـلَى مَـا يَـنْـفَـعُـكَ وَاسْـتَـعِـنْ بِـاللهِ

"Stick to what benefits you and seek Allah's help."

Duaa is to seek Allah's help and to take measures (required for the implementation of whatever needed in question). The servant must follow the legitimate steps to set straight his faith, life and afterlife as mentioned in Quran and Sunnah.

We speak brothers, about the time, and its value. The Duaa I started with is highly suitable to the subject we discuss tonight. Both keeping time saved, and the good consequences that would result in life and afterlife need Allah's help and assistance. If Allah helps you and paves the way for you to keep your time saved and protected from evils, you will benefit from your time. However, if Allah abandons the servant and makes him rely on himself, his time will be in vain and his days will be lost; he will neither benefit from it nor get advantage out of it. So he will come to Allah at the Day of Judgment where his life is spent in vain.

O brothers, to resort to Allah permanently is one of the most important basics in this matter. The Muslim resorts to his Lord the Almighty to set his times right and to fill his times with good deeds and to abstain him from the reasons for wasting time or spending time in what causes pains regarding his religion, life and the Hereafter. The servant should keep closer to Allah and resort to Him in order to be happy in life and the Hereafter. So, there are so many invocations that call for resorting to Allah concerning setting the matters right, saying right, deeds achievement and avoiding mistakes and so on. I beseech Allah to set our times right, to guide us to the straight path and to abstain us from seditions.

LECTURE

Time is a precious treasure in this life, but it is the most valuable one. It comes and will never be back, it is appreciated by the wise people. It is highly cared and regarded to be more valuable than money, house, food, drinks and the like. One of the salaf said about the companions,

أَدْرَكْتُ قَوْماً هُمْ أَحْرَصُ عَلَى وَقْتِهِمْ مِنْكُمْ عَلَى دَنَانِيرِكُمْ

"I saw some people cared for their time more than you cared for your (money) dinars."

They were careful and cautious about their time because time is highly regarded by them, and they realized its value.

When we look through the Quran and the Sunnah, we find many more examples and proofs concerning the value of time and the importance of time-saving that the Muslim should care for. The following are some texts from the Quran and the Sunnah which spot the light on the value of time; I beseech Allah to make it beneficial to us all:

For example: in many verses, Allah the Almighty swears by the parts of time like; Asr, Adduha, Alfajr, the night, the daylight and the like:

﴿ وَٱلۡفَجۡرِ ۝ وَلَيَالٍ عَشۡرٍ ۝ ﴾

"By the Dawn (1) by the ten nights (i.e. the first ten days of the month of Dhul-Hijjah." [*Soorah Al-Fajr* 89:1-2]

And

﴿ وَٱلَّيۡلِ إِذَا يَغۡشَىٰ ۝ وَٱلنَّهَارِ إِذَا تَجَلَّىٰ ۝ ﴾

"By the night as it envelops (1) By the day as it appears in brightness." [*Soorah Al-Layl* 92:1-2]

And

﴿ وَٱلشَّمۡسِ وَضُحَىٰهَا ۝ وَٱلۡقَمَرِ إِذَا تَلَىٰهَا ۝ وَٱلنَّهَارِ إِذَا جَلَّىٰهَا ۝ وَٱلَّيۡلِ إِذَا يَغۡشَىٰهَا ۝ ﴾

"By the sun and its brightness (1) By the moon as it follows it (the sun) (2) By the day as it shows up (the sun's) brightness (3) By the

night as it conceals it (the sun) (4) ."[*Soorah Ash-Shams* 91:1-4]

And

"By the afternoon (after sunrise)) (Soorah Ad-Duha), (By Al-Asr (the time)."[*Soorah Al-Asr* 103:1]

And many other verses from the Holy Quran. Swearing by Allah in these parts of time is an indication of the value of time and how it is important because if Allah swears by his creatures, this is an indication of the greatness of what he has sworn by and its lofty position. Swearing by these parts of time, Al-Fajr, Al-Lail, Al-Asr, Ad-Duha and so on, is a reference that Allah the Almighty highly regards time. It is also important to take care of it as Allah has sworn by it and in which deeds and worships are performed.

The ones who come closer to Allah the Almighty and follow His orders, they perform all of these at particular times, whether in Al-Fajr, Ad-Duha, Al-Asr, Al-Lail or the daylight. These times are highly respected and regarded as it goes and never comes, and any time lost cannot be returned and it is the place of deeds and worships. The time is specified for all kinds of worships, and the successful are the ones who make use of time in worshipping Allah and coming closer to Him. However, the losers waste these fruitful times and limited hours without using it in improving their faith or performing more good deeds or learning more useful knowledge. So, swearing by the different parts of time is a clear evidence of the value of time.

The texts that refer to the value of time and how precious it is: that Allah the Almighty, in many verses considered time and its parts as one of the blessings that are given by Allah in order to be used in worshipping Allah the Almighty, for example; what is mentioned in Soorah An-Nahl, called by some scholars as the Soorah of favors because Allah told about many favors given to His worshippers – in this honorable Soorah Allah says, stating many favors and blessings:

﴿ وَسَخَّرَ لَكُمُ ٱلَّيۡلَ وَٱلنَّهَارَ وَٱلشَّمۡسَ وَٱلۡقَمَرَ وَٱلنُّجُومُ مُسَخَّرَٰتُۢ بِأَمۡرِهِۦٓ إِنَّ فِي ذَٰلِكَ لَأٓيَٰتٍ لِّقَوۡمٍ يَعۡقِلُونَ ۝ ﴾

"And He has subjected to you the night and the day, and His Command subjects the sun

and the moon; and the stars. Surely, in this are proofs for a people who understand." [*Soorah An-Nahl* 16:16]

Allah's statement, **"And He has subjected to the night and the day"** means subjected this time to you, a night comes and a day follows it, and then the night succeeds the day and so on. Day and night, time and hours are subjected to you by Allah the Almighty, of these days and nights, you have a particular time you cannot have a respite for an hour or a moment. In case Allah decrees that you will die at night, you will die before the morning and if Allah decrees that you will die in the morning, you will die before night. So, of days and nights you have particular hours and certain days that will inevitably go away. If it goes away and your days and nights as well, you will pass away. So, some salaf said:

يَا ابْنَ آدَمَ إِنَّمَا أَنْتَ أَيَّام مَعْدُودَة فَانْتَهِي بِانْتِهَاءِ أَيَّامِكَ .

"O son of Adam, you are certain days, and you will finish when they finish."

Allah the Almighty subjected to you day and night and subjected to you all times. He created you when you were not worth mentioning, and He created you at theses times and gave you a particular period because earlier people and nations before us took their share of days and nights. He subjected day and night to them, one of them spent this time worshipping Allah and obeying his orders till his time passed and died, while the others spent their days and nights in performing evil deeds against Allah the Almighty when he comes to his Lord with his days and nights' deeds. Allah the Almighty confers upon his worshippers that he subjected days and nights to them, subjected to you days and nights in life that is your fate in this life and will come to an end.

"For every matter there is a Decree of Allah."
[*Soorah ar-Ra'd* 13:38]

If the man's life ended, his days and nights would finish. And if his life ended, as I said, with a day does not outstrip the night. And his life ended with a night does not exceed the day. This is a great blessing subjected by Allah the Almighty; day, night, the forenoon, Al-Fajr, Al-Asr; these are blessings given by Allah the Almighty. And He created you among these blessings and ordered you to use it in coming closer to Allah the Almighty, So, Allah concluded this verse with saying:

$$\lbrace\ \text{إِنَّ فِى ذَٰلِكَ لَآيَـٰتٍ لِّقَوۡمٍ يَعۡقِلُونَ}\ (١٢)\ \rbrace$$

"Verily, in that are indeed signs for a people who understand."

Whoever use his mind and exploit his thinking and reflect on day and night, sun and moon and the sequence of these times, he will be given a concrete example and a moral lesson, and he will be warned of continuing in mistakes **"Verily, in that are indeed signs."**

Allah the Almighty said:

$$\lbrace\ \text{إِنَّ فِى خَلۡقِ ٱلسَّمَـٰوَٰتِ وَٱلۡأَرۡضِ وَٱخۡتِلَـٰفِ ٱلَّيۡلِ وَٱلنَّهَارِ لَآيَـٰتٍ لِّأُوْلِى ٱلۡأَلۡبَـٰبِ}\ (١٩٠)\ \text{ٱلَّذِينَ يَذۡكُرُونَ ٱللَّهَ قِيَـٰمًا وَقُعُودًا وَعَلَىٰ جُنُوبِهِمۡ وَيَتَفَكَّرُونَ فِى خَلۡقِ ٱلسَّمَـٰوَٰتِ وَٱلۡأَرۡضِ رَبَّنَا مَا خَلَقۡتَ هَـٰذَا بَـٰطِلًا سُبۡحَـٰنَكَ فَقِنَا عَذَابَ ٱلنَّارِ}\ (١٩١)\ \rbrace$$

"Verily in the creation of the heavens and the earth, and in the alternation of night and day, there are indeed signs for men of

understanding. Those who remember Allah (always and in prayers) standing, sitting, and lying down on their sides, and think deeply about the creation of the heavens and the earth, (saying): Our Lord! You have not created (all) this without purpose, glory to You! (Exalted are You, above all, that they associate with You as partners). Give us salvation from the torment of the Fire)." [*Soorah Ali Imran* 3:190-191]

This is the business of the men of understanding, think deeply about the creation of the heavens and the earth, and they think deeply about the alternation of night and day. And the alternation of day and night means their succession, a night came and succeeded by a day, and a day comes succeeded by a night. Allah the Almighty made the alternation of day and night a moral lesson and reminder for the people to use it. If all the time was a night or if all the time were a day, everything would be in a mess and the man will not receive admonition, and he may be bored, lazy and dissatisfied. However, Allah's wisdom in the alternation of day and night is very clear; an activity is renewed with the succession of day and night and the renewal of times. And the alternation of day and night is a reminder and a moral lesson for the men of understanding as Allah the Almighty said:

﴿ وَهُوَ الَّذِي جَعَلَ الَّيْلَ وَالنَّهَارَ خِـلْـفَـةً ﴾

"And He it is Who has put the night and the day in succession," [*Soorah Al-Furqan* 25:62]

Why?

﴿ خِلْفَةً لِّمَنْ أَرَادَ أَن يَذَّكَّرَ أَوْ أَرَادَ شُكُورًا ۝ ﴾

"For such who desires to remember or desires to show his gratitude." [*Soorah Al-Furqan* 25:62]

In succession means a night came and succeeded by a day, a day came and succeeded by a night. So, Allah the Almighty in this order in sequence; a night comes and replaced by a day, a day came and succeeded by a night, why?

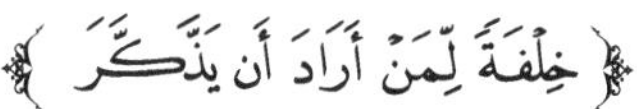

﴿ خِلْفَةً لِّمَنْ أَرَادَ أَن يَذَّكَّرَ ﴾

"For such who desires to remember."

Allah the Almighty made it like this to remember the Greatness of Allah the Almighty, the Greatness of the Creator. Allah the Almighty can make the day continuous till the Day of Resurrection, and to make the night perpetual till the Day of Resurrection. And if Allah the Almighty made the day uninterrupted till the Day of Resurrection, no one can bring daylight in which people can live. And if Allah the Almighty made the day continuous till the Day of Resurrection, no one can bring the night where he or she rest. So, Allah bestowed upon them by making the day and night in succession; a night came and succeeded by a day, and a day came and succeeded by a night. So, days are in succession, why? (for such who desires to remember) This is a fertile way of remembrance, a night gone and a day came, a day went and a night came. So, the man goes ahead in this succeeding days and nights in order to remember Allah the Almighty, the Greatest, the All-Wise and the All-Powerful. And he will remember Allah's orders, to obey Allah and comply with his orders and to abstain from the sins.

"for such who desires to remember or desires to show his gratitude."

Meaning to show gratitude to Allah for this great blessing, the succession of day and night,

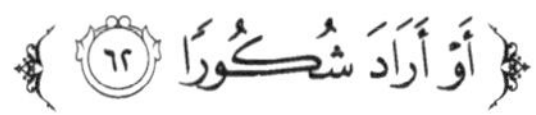

"for such who desires to show his gratitude."

O brothers, I advise you to think about the verse that come after this verse to the end of Surah Al-Furqan,

﴿ وَعِبَادُ ٱلرَّحْمَٰنِ ٱلَّذِينَ يَمْشُونَ عَلَى ٱلْأَرْضِ هَوْنًا وَإِذَا خَاطَبَهُمُ ٱلْجَٰهِلُونَ قَالُوا سَلَٰمًا ﴿٦٣﴾ ﴾

"And the faithful slaves of the Most Gracious (Allah) are those who walk on the earth in humility and sedateness, and the foolish address them (with bad words) they reply back with mild words of gentleness." [*Soorah Al-Furqan* 25:63]

Allah the Almighty mentioned the traits of the slaves of the Most Gracious (Allah) who remember Allah within the succession of days and nights and the alternation of day and night, they remember Allah, so they do not spare effort to obey Allah and they work to come closer to Allah and they abstain from the sins.

Of the texts of the Quran that express the value of time: what Allah said in verses about those who waste their time in disbelief, disobedience, abhorrence, oppression and abstaining from Allah the Almighty. Those mentioned before are greatly sorry for many times they lost and many days they wasted. And they beseech Allah to send them back to life for making good deeds, to make up for their life that they lost. This is far reached. Whoever waste time in this life, cannot be sent back to life to obey Allah the Almighty. So, in many ayat, those who lost time in disobeying Allah, they feel regretful. And Allah the Almighty warned the worshippers in many ayat from the Quran: Allah said:

﴿ يَـٰٓأَيُّهَا ٱلَّذِينَ ءَامَنُوا۟ لَا تُلْهِكُمْ أَمْوَٰلُكُمْ وَلَآ أَوْلَـٰدُكُمْ عَن ذِكْرِ ٱللَّهِ وَمَن يَفْعَلْ ذَٰلِكَ فَأُو۟لَـٰٓئِكَ هُمُ ٱلْخَـٰسِرُونَ ۝ وَأَنفِقُوا۟ مِن مَّا رَزَقْنَـٰكُم مِّن قَبْلِ أَن يَأْتِىَ أَحَدَكُمُ ٱلْمَوْتُ فَيَقُولَ رَبِّ لَوْلَآ أَخَّرْتَنِىٓ إِلَىٰٓ أَجَلٍ قَرِيبٍ فَأَصَّدَّقَ وَأَكُن مِّنَ ٱلصَّـٰلِحِينَ ۝ ﴾

"O you who believe! Let not your properties or your children divert you from the remembrance of Allah. And whosoever does that, then they are the losers. And spend (in charity) of that with which We have provided you before death comes to one of you, and he says: "My Lord! If only You would give me respite for a little while (i.e. return to the worldly life), then I should give Sadaqah (i.e. Zakat of my wealth), and be among the

righteous {i.e. perform Hajj (pilgrimage to Makkah) and other good deeds." [*Soorah Al-Munafiqun 63:9-10*]

And when death comes, the one who lost his time will beseech Allah the Almighty to respite them to a short period, a short period of time, to do righteous deeds, to obey Allah the Almighty,

$$﴿ إِلَىٰٓ أَجَلٍ قَرِيبٍ فَأَصَّدَّقَ وَأَكُن مِّنَ ٱلصَّٰلِحِينَ ۝ ﴾$$

"for a little while (i.e. return to the worldly life), then I should give Sadaqah (i.e. Zakat of my wealth), and be among the righteous {i.e. perform Hajj (pilgrimage to Makkah) and other good deeds." [*Soorah Al-Munafiqun 63:10*]

Meaning to be at that time one of the righteous, the charitable, the obedient and the ones who obey Allah's orders,

$$﴿ لَوْلَآ أَخَّرْتَنِىٓ إِلَىٰٓ أَجَلٍ قَرِيبٍ ﴾$$

"If only You would give me respite for a little while) he asks for a respite."

What is the answer?

$$\{ \text{وَلَن يُؤَخِّرَ ٱللَّهُ نَفْسًا إِذَا جَآءَ أَجَلُهَا ۚ وَٱللَّهُ خَبِيرٌۢ بِمَا تَعْمَلُونَ} \ (١١) \}$$

"And Allah grants respite to none when his appointed time (death) comes. And Allah is Well-Acquainted with what you do." [*Soorah Al-Munafiqun* 63:11]

Whomever his death comes and his life comes to an end, if he asks to be granted a respite for a minute, he will not be given.

In this context, it is worth mentioning to say that when Al-Hassan Al-Basri (may Allah give him mercy) was at a funeral, he said to a man beside him, after burial:

"If you were in the place of the dead, what would you like?" He said: I wish Allah sent me back to life again to do righteous deeds not that (evil deeds) I used to do. Al-Hassan said: "Now your request is implemented, so, go ahead."

So, now you have much more time and strength to do good deeds, but when he is dead, and his spirit is caught, he wishes and beseeches Allah the Almighty to send him back to life and gives him a respite for a little while to perform good deeds. Though he is not answered, and his good deeds are not accepted. And

,at the Day of Judgment, when the people of fire enter hellfire- may Allah keep us away from the hellfire- they are crying and screaming in hell fire, and asking Allah the Almighty to send them back to life to do righteous good deeds and obey Allah's orders but no way.

Allah the Almighty said:

﴿ وَٱلَّذِينَ كَفَرُوا۟ لَهُمْ نَارُ جَهَنَّمَ لَا يُقْضَىٰ عَلَيْهِمْ فَيَمُوتُوا۟ وَلَا يُخَفَّفُ عَنْهُم مِّنْ عَذَابِهَا كَذَٰلِكَ نَجْزِى كُلَّ كَفُورٍ ۝ وَهُمْ يَصْطَرِخُونَ فِيهَا رَبَّنَا أَخْرِجْنَا نَعْمَلْ صَٰلِحًا غَيْرَ ٱلَّذِى كُنَّا نَعْمَلُ ﴾

"But those who disbelieve (in the Oneness of Allah – Islamic Monotheism), for them, will be the Fire of Hell. Neither will it have a complete killing effect on them so that they die nor shall its torment be lightened for them. Thus do We requite every disbeliever! Within they will cry: Our Lord! Bring us out, we shall do righteous good deeds, not (the evil deeds) that we used to do." [*Soorah Fatir* 35:36-37]

This is what they say when they are in hellfire,

$$\lbrace\ \text{رَبَّنَآ أَخْرِجْنَا نَعْمَلْ صَلِحًا غَيْرَ ٱلَّذِى كُنَّا نَعْمَلُ}\ \rbrace$$

"Our Lord! Bring us out, we shall do righteous good deeds, not (the evil deeds) that we used to do." [*Soorah Fatir* 35:37]

Meaning O' Allah give us a new chance, send us back to life again to do righteous good deeds, not (the evil deeds) that we used to do in life (i.e. disbelief, oppression, abhorrence, and disobedience) (shall do righteous good deeds, not (the evil deeds) that we used to do) what is the reply? (Allah will answer):

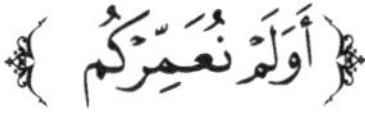

$$\lbrace\ \text{أَوَلَمْ نُعَمِّرْكُم}\ \rbrace$$

"Did We not give you lives long enough,"

Meaning in life.

$$\lbrace\ \text{مَا يَتَذَكَّرُ فِيهِ مَن تَذَكَّرَ وَجَآءَكُمُ ٱلنَّذِيرُ فَذُوقُوا۟ فَمَا لِلظَّٰلِمِينَ مِن نَّصِيرٍ ٣٧}\ \rbrace$$

"So that whosoever would receive admonition could receive it? And the warner came to you. So taste you (the evil of your deeds), For the Zalimun (polytheists and wrongdoers) there is no helper." [*Soorah Al-Fatir* 35:37]

This is their case in Hellfire; they are crying because of wasting time in life. And we are still, many thanks to Allah, at the time of deeds performing in life.

The doors of obedience are open, the ways of goodness are allowed and the signs of guidance are clear. Good deeds are to be done, laziness and idleness to left. And everyone should seriously and actively come closer to Allah.

Of the texts that are mentioned in the Sunnah regarding the value of time and being a great blessing many people lose. The Prophet (ﷺ) said (Saheeh Al-Bukhari):

نِعْمَتَانِ مَغْبُونٌ فِيهِمَا كَثِيرٌ مِنَ النَّاسِ :
الصِّحَّةُ وَالْفَرَاغُ

"There are two blessings in which many people incur loss: health and free time for doing good."

Many people incur loss concerning these two blessings; they suffer loss as they lose them all, and they do not obtain the good, righteous deeds.

نِـعْمَتَانِ مَغْبُـونٌ فِـيهِـمَا كَثِـيرٌ مِـنَ النَّـاسِ :
الـصِّـحَّـةُ وَالْـفَـرَاغُ

"There are two blessings in which many people suffer loss: health and free time for doing good."

Many people, particularly the young men, are given health. The young are in good health and vitality, but most of them waste this youth, health and vitality in playing and amusement. Moreover, some ask the other to join him for killing and wasting time. Frankly speaking, they call each other **"let's kill time"**, they said like this: **"let's kill time, waste time."**

Phrases said by many refer to significant loss and apparent deception, the state in which many young people live; killing time and wasting life in vain. However, they often misuse time in things that have a bad effect on the servant in life and the Hereafter.

For the Muslim, time is so valuable that not to be killed. Can anyone kill someone he loves? Can anyone waste something valuable to him? Absolutely not. Thus, those do not realize the value of time, they do not look upon it, they do not know its value. So they kill it without a knife, and they waste it and they agreed to waste it and kill it, **"Let's kill time"**, **"Let's waste time."**

Is this the right Muslim? Is this the knowledgeable Muslim who realizes that he will die and will be questioned? How can he kill time and waste it? What else? If he stands before Allah, he will be asked concerning his time. Allah will surely ask you about your time. The Prophet (ﷺ) reported:

لَا تَزُولُ قَدَمَا عَبْدٍ يَوْمَ الْقِيَامَةِ حَتَّى يُسْأَلَ عَنْ

أَرْبَعِ خِصَالٍ : عَنْ عُمُرِهِ فِيمَا أَفْنَاهُ ؟ وَ عَنْ

شَبَابِهِ فِيمَا أَبْلَاهُ ؟ وَ عَنْ مَالِهِ مِنْ أَيْنَ اكْتَسَبَهُ

وَ فِيمَا أَنْفَقَهُ ؟ وَ عَنْ عِلْمِهِ مَاذَا عَمِلَ فِيهِ .

"Man's feet will not move on the Day of Resurrection before he is asked about four aspects: his life, how did he consume it, his youth, how did he wear it out, his wealth, how did he earn it and how did he dispose of it, and, about his knowledge, what did he do with it."

These are four questions asked to every one of us in the Day of Resurrection. No man's feet will move on the Day of Resurrection before he is asked about four aspects, he started with the life,

عَنْ عُمُرِهِ فِيـمَا أَفْنَاهُ؟

"his life, how did he consume it."

This is a question about time, the first and second questions in this hadith are about time

عَنْ عُمُرِهِ فِيـمَا أَفْنَاهُ، وَ عَنْ شَبَابِهِ فِيـمَا أَبْلَاهُ؟

"his life, how did he consume it, his youth, how did he wear it out?"

Although the youth is part of man's life, everyone specially asked about it on the Day of Resurrection. The man is asked about all his life, how did he consume it, and about his youth, how did he wear it out, even if it is part of his life, why? The scholars said: because youth is strength between two weaknesses: the weakness of childhood and the weakness of senility. Youth is the stage of strength, activity, enthusiasm and determination. How can anyone waste all of these?

Even Allah asks the man about his youth. In the Day of Resurrection he will be told, you were energetic and healthy what did you do?

What did you perform? How did you obey your Lord? How did you make proper use your time? He will be asked about his life in general and his youth in particular. And then he will be asked about his wealth and his knowledge. This highlights the value of time and caring for it, and that everyone will be asked concerning his time on the Day of Resurrection.

In another hadith, the Prophet (ﷺ) urged everyone to make use of time before going away; the Prophet (ﷺ):

اِغْتَنِمْ خَمْسًا قَبْلَ خَمْسٍ : شَبَابَكَ قَبْلَ هِرَامِكَ ، وَ صِحَّتَكَ قَبْلَ سَقَمِكَ ، وَ غِنَاءَكَ قَبْلَ فَقْرِكَ ، وَ فَرَاغَكَ قَبْلَ شُغْلِكَ ، وَ حَيَاتَكَ قَبْلَ مَوْتِكَ .

"Make good use of five matters before five things would happen: Make good use of your life before your death, your good health before you get ill, your youth before you get old, your good wealth before you get poor, and your spare time before you get pre-occupied." "Your spare time before you get pre-occupied."

This is about time.

وَ فَرَاغَكَ قَبْلَ شُغْلِكَ

"Your spare time before you get pre-occupied."

Everyone has much more time what did he do to make good use of it? The Prophet (ﷺ) said that you should make good use of spare time before you get pre-occupied **"Five matters before five things"** one of these **"Your spare time before you get pre-occupied"**, the spare time in man's life is an excellent opportunity to obey Allah, if you mentioned in spare time,

سُبْحَانَ اللهِ وَ بِحَمْدِهِ

"Glory be to Allah, Most Great and Worthy of Praise" one time, a palm tree will be planted for you in paradise, what is the matter if you mentioned this Dhikr hundred times! One hundred palm trees. This remembrance of Allah is the planting of paradise as authenticated by the Prophet (ﷺ). How many hours do we waste, and how many times we do not make proper use of or build our real life, the Day of Resurrection,

﴿ وَإِنَّ ٱلدَّارَ ٱلْأَخِرَةَ لَهِيَ ٱلْحَيَوَانُ لَوْ كَانُوا۟ يَعْلَمُونَ ۝ ﴾

"Verily, the home of the Hereafter – that is the life indeed (i.e. the eternal life that will never end), if they but know." [*Soorah Al-Ankabut* 29:64]

The Prophet (ﷺ) urged us to make good use of that. Make proper use of the youth period; the state of many people regarding time and life is procrastination and delay. This is the actual waste of time. Many young people are as such: when he is told to obey and abstain from sins, he says, **"I am still young, I can do later."** Does the youth mean to waste time and lose his life? Alternatively, does the youth expect to make good use of time in the state of vitality, power, determination, hard working, energy, obeying Allah's orders and doing righteous good deeds?

﴿ وَٱلَّذِينَ جَٰهَدُوا۟ فِينَا لَنَهْدِيَنَّهُمْ سُبُلَنَا وَإِنَّ ٱللَّهَ لَمَعَ ٱلْمُحْسِنِينَ ۝ ﴾

"And for those who strive hard in Us (Our Cause), We will surely guide them to Our Paths (i.e. Allah's religion – Islamic

Monotheism). And verily, Allah is with the Muhsinin (good-doers ." [*Soorah Al-Ankabut* 29:69]

The young people should make good use of his youth and the healthy should make proper use of his health.

Once upon a time, I saw a young man in one of the hospitals, he is twenty years old or a little older. When I saw him, his body is burnt a year before I saw him. I saw him a year after being burnt. All his body is wholly consumed as if it was a piece of charred wood; his hand is indurated, his foot is so indurated and pale that he cannot move, and he is lying in bed for a year. A young man is in his twenties. This young man is thinking a lot about types of worships and means of nearness. And you are in good health and energy. I saw a Mushaf (the Holy Quran) in front of this young man; I said how can you recite? He told me that when I need to take this Mushaf I asked them to open it in front of me. He cannot open it himself because his hand is indurated, so Al-Mushaf is opened, and he starts reciting. And he calls someone to turn the page over when it is finished. Your hand is activated; your insight is good, and so is your health. So do you go through the pages of the Mushaf? Do you think about the words of Allah? To what you are energetic in obeying Allah and making righteous good deeds?!

Concerning the handicapped, who is the handicapped really, the handicapped really is not the one who lost his leg or hand or any of his organs. The handicapped really is the healthy one but disabled to obey Allah, he has two legs, he has two hands, he has two eyes, he is in good health but he is disabled to obey Allah, this is really the handicapped. However, who lost his foot, hand, eyesight or hearing, but he does righteous good deeds as possible as he can; this is not handicapped. The handicapped is the one who is disabled to obey and who is deprived of worshipping Allah.

Before many years, I saw a man lost his leg cut from the knee, he has only one leg, he was praying Tarawih with one leg only and put the stick aside. He clearly stands relying on one leg praying Taraweeh. And in the past they were performing Al-Taraweeh or Tahajjud in Al-Masjid Nabawi with three Juz and a half late at night, so the prayerful got tired. I surely saw him with my own eyes and in front of me praying Al-Tahajjud with three Juz and a half on one leg. This is not handicapped even if his leg is lost. The handicapped is the one who is sitting on the street, with two legs and two hands, but he does not make use of them in obeying Allah and coming closer to Him.

The Prophet (ﷺ) advised us:

اِغْتَنِمْ خَمْسًا قَبْلَ خَمْسٍ

"Make good use of five matters before five things would happen."

And making use of time is in the past time, it is said make good use of it, because if it is gone, the profit has gone, if it is gone, the spoils are gone. Thus, the man needs to make proper use of matters, do the youth come back if it is gone? No, it does not! So, the man makes good use of it before it is gone. To make proper use of health before it is gone, to make good use of vitality before it is gone. And to make use of time before it is gone for obeying Allah the Almighty and coming closer to Allah.

So, the texts that indicate the value of time is so much. If we think deeply about these texts, there is a good lesson we need to study together: how can anyone keep his time saved?

But I want to convey a message of Al-Fudayl Bin Eyad, a fruitful dialog between AL-Fudayl Bin Eyad and a man at the age of sixty. Al-Fudayl Bin Eyad met him and had a productive dialog with him. Al-Fudayl Bin Eyad said to someone: how old are you? He answered: sixty. He said:

فَأَنْتَ مُنْذُ سِتَّيـنَ سِنَّةً تَـسِـيـرُ إِلَى رَبِّكَ ، يُـوشِـكُ
أَنْ تَبْـلُـغَ .

"You were going ahead to your Lord sixty years ago; you are about to reach."

Meaning your time is about to come to an end in this life. The man said: **"to Allah we belong, to Him we shall return."** Al-Fudayl Bin Eyad said: **"do you know its interpretation? Do you know the meaning of what you said?"** And, by the way, many Adhkār such as: to Allah we belong, to Him we shall return, there is not power but in Allah or Glory be to Allah or so mentioned by many people but if he asked about its meaning, they do not know. Thus, this a noteworthy remark by Al-Fudayl Bin Eyad, he said to him: **"do you know its interpretation?"** Meaning, you said: **"to Allah we belong, to Him we shall return. Do you know the definition of this word?"** Then he started explaining the meaning of this word, listen to the explanation: you say I am a servant of

Allah this means **"to Allah we belong"**: I am a servant of Allah and to Him I shall return. The word **"to Allah we belong, to Him we shall return"** is made up of two sentences: the first one is acknowledgement of worship of Allah by the slave **"to Allah we belong"**: meaning, I am a servant of Allah, I am a slave, I am created by Allah, I am created for worshipping, Allah is my Lord, this is the first sentence **"to Allah we belong"** meaning to Allah we belong, Allah created us and caused us to exist and conduct us. The other sentence **"to Allah we shall return"** meaning all of us will return to Allah, none will stay in this life,

"And that to your Lord (Allah) is the end (Return of everything)." [*Soorah An-Najm* 53:42]

"Surely, to your Lord is the return." [*Soorah Al-'Alq* 96:8]

So, the return and the end are to Allah the Almighty. To Allah we belong, to Him we shall return. Al-Fudayl said that it meant:

"I am a servant of Allah and to Him I shall return. So, whoever know that he is a servant of Allah to Him he shall return, he will know that he will stand, in front of Allah. And whoever know that he will stand in front of Allah, he surely knows that he will be questioned. And whoever know that he is questioned, he shall prepare an answer."

This is an explanation by Al-Fudayl, may Allah have mercy on him, of **"to Allah we belong and to Allah we shall return."** What did the man say when this clear explanation is given to him, and he understands apparently the meaning of this word? He said: what can we do? Al-Fudayl said to him, **"It is an easy task."** The man said: **"What is it?"** He said: **"If you do righteous good deeds in the coming days, your last days will be forgiven."** Allah is the greatest! This is the grace of Allah and a great blessing of Allah; sixty years are lost then he asks what to do? He said: **"if you do righteous good deeds in the coming days, your last days will be forgiven."** We have heard Allah said:

﴿ ۞ قُلْ يَـٰعِبَادِىَ ٱلَّذِينَ أَسْرَفُوا۟ عَلَىٰٓ أَنفُسِهِمْ لَا تَقْنَطُوا۟ مِن رَّحْمَةِ ٱللَّهِ إِنَّ ٱللَّهَ يَغْفِرُ ٱلذُّنُوبَ جَمِيعًا إِنَّهُۥ هُوَ ٱلْغَفُورُ ٱلرَّحِيمُ ۝ ﴾

"Say: O Ibadi (My slaves) who have transgressed against themselves (by committing evil deeds and sins)! Despair not of the Mercy of Allah: verily, Allah forgives all sins. Truly He is Oft-Forgiving, Most Merciful." [*Soorah Az-Zumar* 39:53]

So, in another saying by one of the salaf said:

"Do you know what the cold spoils are? The cold spoils mean if you do righteous good deeds in the coming days, your last days will be forgiven."

If all that happened in the past is abhorrence and disobedience, do righteous good deeds in the coming days, your last days will be forgiven.

﴿إِن يَنتَهُواْ يُغْفَرْ لَهُم مَّا قَدْ سَلَفَ﴾

"If they cease (from disbelief) their past will be forgiven." [*Soorah Al-Anfal* 8:38]

Islam forgives what is done before it, and repentance forgives what is done before it. This is a blessing of Allah the Almighty. Thus, none shall despair of the Mercy of Allah:

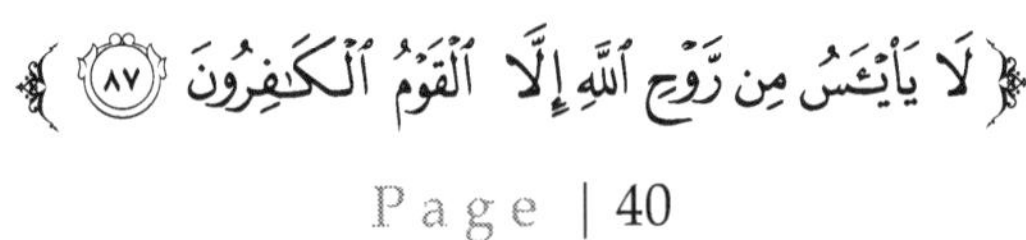

"Certainly, no one despairs of Allah's Mercy, except the people who disbelieve." [*Soorah Yusuf* 12:87]

So, the servant shall make proper use of the coming days, what is happened in your life ended. If it is obedience, be grateful to Allah, and if it is sin, ask for Allah's forgiveness. Allah the Almighty said,

﴿ يَقْبَلُ ٱلتَّوْبَةَ عَنْ عِبَادِهِۦ وَيَعْفُواْ عَنِ ٱلسَّيِّئَاتِ ﴾

"And He it is Who accepts repentance from His slaves, and forgives sins." [*Soorah Ash-Shura* 42:25]

He said: **"if you do righteous good deeds in the coming days, your last days will be forgiven, so, in case you do evil deeds in the coming days, the coming and the past days will be lost."** Thus, the servant shall get the cold spoils. Whomever his time is lost, and his days are wasted.

Whoever wasted his past time, the kinds of good deeds are available, and the ways of goodness are clear. He shall start his way by asking for Allah's forgiveness for every sin and come to Allah with energy and determination. Allah said:

﴿ وَالَّذِينَ جَاهَدُوا فِينَا لَنَهْدِيَنَّهُمْ سُبُلَنَا وَإِنَّ اللَّهَ لَمَعَ الْمُحْسِنِينَ ۝ ﴾

"As for those who strive hard in Us (Our Cause), We will surely guide them to Our Paths (i.e. Allah's religion – Islamic Monotheism). And verily, Allah is with the Muhsinun (good-doers)." [*Soorah Al-Ankabut* 29:69]

At last we will speak about how to keep time saved. And I will tackle this issue in main points because there is no enough time:

First: to seek Allah's Help, to depend on Him and to resort to Him in order to save anyone's time and to keep him away from seditions. The Prophet (ﷺ) said:

اللَّهُمَّ لَكَ أَسْلَمْتُ وَ بِكَ آمَنْتُ وَ عَلَيْكَ تَوَكَّلْتُ وَ إِلَيْكَ أَنَبْتُ وَ بِكَ خَاصَمْتُ ، اللَّهُمَّ إِنِّي أَعُوذُ بِعِزَّتِكَ لَا إِلَهَ إِلَّا أَنْتَ أَنْ تُضِلَّنِي أَنْتَ الْحَيُّ الَّذِي لَا يَمُوتُ وَ الْجِنُّ وَ الْإِنْسُ يَمُوتُونَ .

"O Allah, I submit my face to You, I believe in You, and I rely upon You, and to You I will return, with **Your Help I contend my adversaries and from You I seek judgment. O' Allah, I seek refuge with Your Grandeur, none has the right to be worshipped but You, to be led astray, You are the Ever Living one who never dies, but the Jinn and the man will inevitably die."** [Related by *Muslim in Saheeh*]

<u>**The first**</u> thing that the man shall do is to resort to Allah the Almighty.

<u>**Second**</u>: to beseech Allah's forgiveness for every sin and to sincerely repent,

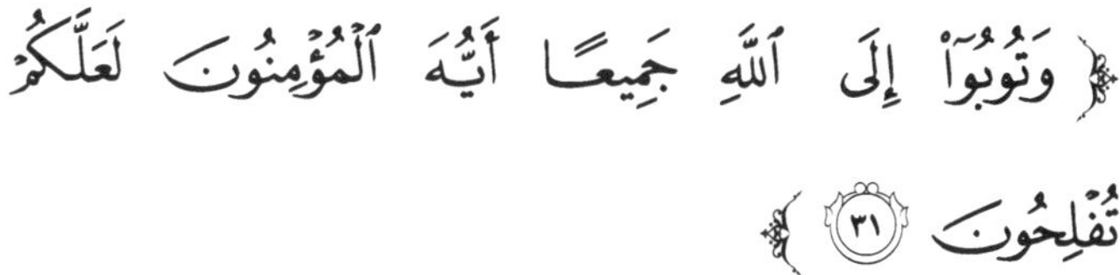

﴿ وَتُوبُوٓاْ إِلَى ٱللَّهِ جَمِيعًا أَيُّهَ ٱلْمُؤْمِنُونَ لَعَلَّكُمْ تُفْلِحُونَ ٣١ ﴾

"And all of you beg Allah to forgive you all, O believers, that you may be successful." [*Soorah An-Nur* 24:31]

This is the way to success.

﴿ يَٰٓأَيُّهَا ٱلَّذِينَ ءَامَنُواْ تُوبُوٓاْ إِلَى ٱللَّهِ تَوْبَةً نَّصُوحًا ﴾

"O you who believe! Turn to Allah with sincere repentance." [*Soorah At-Tahreem* 66:8]

A sincere repentance from sins and offenses is to repent for every evil deed, to abandon it totally, and to be decisive not to do it again. This is the real repentance.

And then to strive hard to obey Allah and to come closer to Him with what gratify him. And the requisites of Islam are the best thing to being done to come closer to Allah. Allah said in Divine Hadith:

وَ مَا تَقَرَّبَ إِلَيَّ عَبْدِي بِشَيْءٍ أَحَبَّ إِلَيَّ مِمَّا افْتَرَضْتُ عَلَيْهِ.

"There is nothing makes coming closer to Allah better than the requisites of Allah."

So, the most important thing after Tawheed is to keep performing prayers.

Anyway, this is the conclusion.

NOTES

NOTES

NOTES